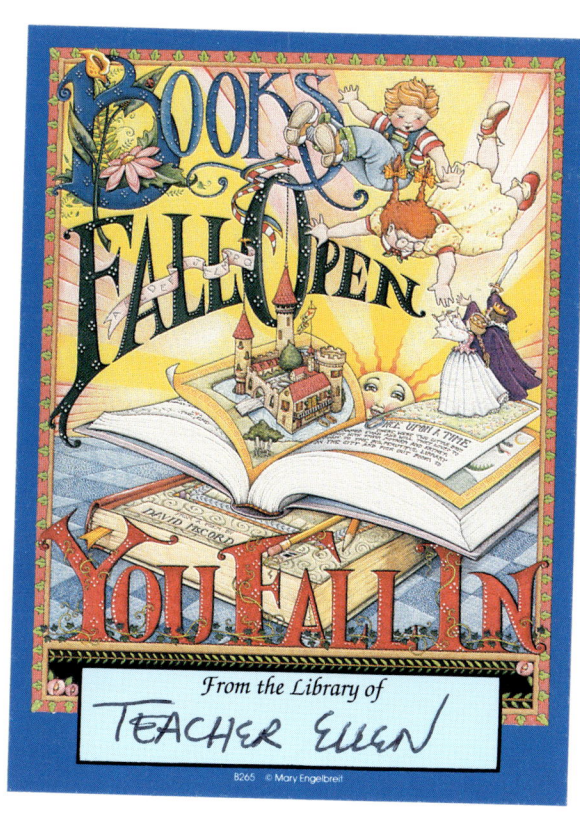

The Magic Word

by George Poppel

Illustrated by Barry Moyer

National Press, Inc.
7508 Wiconsin Avenue
Bethesda, Maryland 20814

(301) 657-1616

The Magic Word
by George Poppel
Illustrated by Barry Moyer
©National Press, Inc. 1986
7508 Wisconsin Avenue
Bethesda, Maryland 20814
(301) 657-1616
All rights reserved.

Library of Congress Cataloging in Publication Data

```
Poppel, George 1948-
   The magic word

(Pandamonium book)

   Summary: Emphasizes in rhyme the importance and
advantages of using the word "please."
   1.  Etiquette for children and youth.  (Etiquette).
I.  Title.

BJ1857.C5P67   1986       395-.122      86-12545
ISBN 0-915765-31-4
```

Dedication

This book is dedicated to Arlene Singer, mother of our two young sons who occasionally have trouble remembering the magic word.

There's a magic word

that you should know.

It has six little letters

to make things go.

It puts on your shirt

and gets you a drink.

It's a very magic word.

What do you think?

The magic word

helps you cross the street.

You can go there magically

without moving your feet.

The word isn't "open sesame,"

but it can open doors.

It will give you a lift

when doing your chores.

The word isn't "waiter,"

but it will get you a treat.

If you are thirsty or hungry

it brings you something to eat.

It carries you on shoulders

over rocks and big boulders.

It will build you a kite

and tuck you in for the night.

It takes you to the circus,

the movies and the zoo.

It isn't red, it isn't white

and it surely isn't blue.

When you wake up in the morning

and you want your favorite O's,

use the magic word

that everybody knows.

It turns on a light when its dark outside.

And it takes you out for a Sunday ride.

The word isn't "give me" or "buy me" or "bring me."

It sure isn't "get me" or "take me" or "gimme."

If you haven't guessed,

I'll have to tell you.

The word is "Please."

I'm sure that you knew.

But in case you forget,

or get a forgetful disease,

please rhymes with trees and

with peas and with cheese.

When you say please

and someone does you a favor,

say "thank you very much"

and they will think you are clever.

"Thank you" is a magic word too.

Say it and nice things happen to you.

So don't forget what you've learned today.

"Please" and "thank you" are magic to say.

Use them and good things will soon come your way.